*Come Stroll With Me
Along The
Pathway of Words*

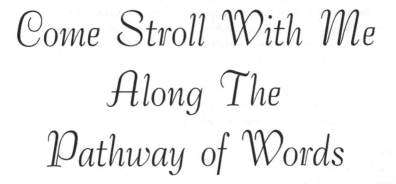

Come Stroll With Me Along The Pathway of Words

Wendy Brooks

COME STROLL WITH ME ALONG THE PATHWAY OF WORDS

iUniverse books may be ordered through booksellers or by contacting:

iUniverse
1663 Liberty Drive
Bloomington, IN 47403
www.iuniverse.com
844-349-9409

ISBN: 978-1-6632-5899-1 (sc)
ISBN: 978-1-6632-5898-4 (e)

Library of Congress Control Number: 2023923937

Print information available on the last page.

iUniverse rev. date: 12/20/2023

Acknowledgment

As God loved me he gave me my wonderful family. They fill my heart with love and joy. They are always ready to help me when help is needed. My life would not be complete without them, and I thank them every day with all my heart.

Contents

A Kindred Spirit

Aches and Pains

Aches and pains, are they part of your everyday life?

Do they drag your spirits lower and lower as the days move slowly along?

Do you see a light at the end of the tunnel, or is it only a long, dark passageway with no answers?

Are you willing to accept this fate, or can you fight for a healthier existence?

Add a new member to my medical team, study my health problems for further information,

Involve myself more fully in my condition, if I haven't involved myself before.

All of this with a positive attitude toward my healing for a happier future for myself.

Whatever time I am given, let me use it to the betterment of my health!

A Blessing

I saw a blessing today!

As I was waiting in line at a fast-food restaurant, I saw a customer defend the worker behind the counter.

The customer's order had been incorrectly filled, and the manager was determined to blame the employee. The customer, who was a frequent visitor, told him that the equipment didn't seem to be working correctly as it had happened frequently in the past week.

Most people would have said nothing, but this individual stood up and told the truth.

This is an example of how we might rise to the occasion and help our world be a better place.

One small voice for humanity!

Multiply this occurrence by millions, and what a wonderful world we would have.

So watch for the chances to serve!

They are there!

A Full Life

I should have known when you were born in such a hurry that all through

Life, you would never tarry.

For you would run nonstop through each day.

Enjoying whatever comes your way.

Experiencing life to its fullest whether in your job, your friendships, or your family,

Always involved with your heart, no matter what the situation.

And when night falls, as sure as clockwork, your running stops.

Time to recharge for you need the peace of the night, the strength of rest to

Enable your continued love of life.

God has given you this wonderful body, inquisitive mind, and dynamic personality.

Heed the signs, obey your instincts, and live life fully as you were meant to live!

A Kindred Spirit

Have you met the person who thinks like you?
Who opens their mouth to speak and sounds like you,
A person whose arguments over politics, debates on moral issues, or opinions
On life's values mirrors your own?
It is almost as though you are hearing yourself as they speak.
If they are already your friend, what a wonderful gift you have been given.
If they are not currently a friend, consider the possibility of such a friendship
And cultivate that relationship.
It could lead to many hours of sharing and pleasant memories of finding a kindred spirit.

A Kind Act

A single moment!

What opportunity is open to us in a single moment?

What can we do, and who can we touch in that moment of time?

Consider the occasions that present themselves to us.

The grocery store employee who is searching for an item for me.

We begin to talk, and she tells me of her problems.

As we leave each other, we smile, better because we had that single moment.

A drugstore clerk who was tallying my items and spoke of his recent unexpected illness and shared his story with me.

A single moment to care about another's life.

Be open to the possibilities, and when it happens, be ready to listen and share.

A single moment of togetherness as God intended.

A Smile

What a difference it can make if you can frame a smile for those you meet.

If you can say, "Hello," with warmth in your voice and sincerity in your manner,

You will make another's day.

Erase the gloom they might be feeling, and turn their day into a better day!

Such a little task, but do you realize what you might accomplish?

Erase a sadness lodged inside, and lighten a pain-filled life for a moment in time.

It will be a selfless act; no proof will you have that a difference was made.

But what is God's plan?

"Complete our tasks and travel on."

An ambassador of goodwill we will be.

An Old Soul

Have you heard the expression, "An old soul"?

Someone who, even from the earliest stage of their life, seems to have a maturity that doesn't match their age.

Someone who would make comments that would make you stop and look at them and wonder, *Did that come out of their mouth?*

An attitude of peace deep inside that governs their lives,

Where did this come from?

One of the mysteries of life, I presume to say.

In this universe of ours, there is still the unknown, which scholars, scientists, and explorers will continue searching the land for the answers.

An old soul is one of those mysteries.

Enjoy the wonder; marvel at each and every occurrence.

Another gift in our existence.

Balance in Life

What does it mean to have a balance in your life?

Is your life divided in equal parts by the minute and the hour?

That would be balance but impossible to accomplish.

Does it mean we have to have equal parts of work and leisure?

Again, most unlikely that could occur.

Basically, balance is not an easy goal to accomplish.

We all know the workaholic or the lazy bum, where do we fit in this picture?

Do we pay attention to how we are using our days?

This is probably one of the most important tasks we are given. And sadly enough, something that we don't think about enough.

We have to do the work; we have to do the balancing.

Work, family, leisure time, chores, and solitude all needed to refresh the soul.

Being aware is the most important part of this equation.

For if we are aware, we can commit to balancing our lives.

Believe in Yourself

There is nothing more important than the statement, "Believe in yourself."

Put aside all those nagging thoughts: *I'm not handsome or pretty enough; I have no personality; I'm not smart enough.*

Each of us is unique in our own ways.

Do not compare yourself to others; let your own attributes shine.

Maybe your personality is quiet; maybe you like to be alone and find it difficult to make friends.

These are not negatives unless you allow them to be.

Stop agonizing over these feelings; put them in a box, and bury them as deeply as you can.

This can bring you the freedom to be as God wants you—only you—to be.

Now, these thoughts will try to arise from the hole you placed them in, but when you feel that

Happening, squelch that thought right away by thinking positive thoughts.

Praise yourself for the traits and talents that you have.

Praise yourself for the dreams and plans that you are contemplating.

This strength is there, waiting for you to draw it forward.

Meet the challenge; do not be the slave.

Be the master of your life.

Believers

There are so many wonderful people who live in this world, who have God's heart beating in their chest.

They are called in numerous ways, in different causes to show God's kindness and love.

Sometimes in these days of confusion and strife, we don't realize how many still strive to exhibit the peace and calm that marks God's love.

Believers who share the love for others in each and every day

In small ways with a smile and caring touch;

In large ways with time, money, and dedication to the betterment of all.

Do not ever believe that God's love is less in any way because it will always be there for those who have opened their heart to let God in.

Those willing to be available to show God's love in whatever way God leads them, wherever he sees a need, and shares that need with us.

Thank you, God, for allowing us to be aware with the betterment of all as our goals.

We will always be alert and ready to follow God's direction.

Blessings

Do we deserve the blessings that God gives us?

Well, let me ask,

How long will it take for your answer?

I imagine not too long at all because the truth is, none of us deserve his blessings.

They are freely given to us with all his love and his hope that we will act on those blessings.

So what do we do with the blessings?

Do we make good use of them, or do we squander them away, wasting the opportunities that have presented themselves to us?

The blessings that we should be sharing, making someone's life better.

How blessed we are to carry God's plan to another?

To be able to enjoy the dreams that come true.

To be God's ambassador of joy.

Books

What a privilege we are given to have books to read.

Books that educate us in a number of ways.

Books that entertain us with fact or fiction.

Books that take us out of our shells and into the world.

Written in many languages, accommodating whatever your nationality, and

In big print for those whose sight is limited.

Whether the topic be in education, entertainment, history, or the joy of make-believe,

All ways give us so much pleasure.

Thanks to the authors of this world who conduct research in nature, science, history, philosophy, mathematics, all to enlighten us and give us knowledge for our own uses.

Thanks to the authors who write fiction, giving us comedy, adventure, romance, mystery, and science fiction, all allowing us to be out of our world into the world of the fantasies that entertain us. A break from the everyday trials and problems!

Although technology is leading us into another direction, don't forget the pleasure of

Curling up in a chair, wrapped in a blanket, and becoming a part of the novel that consumes us.

Delightful entertainment!

Priced fairly!

Always available!

What more could we ask for?

Keep writing, authors, because my world would be a very unhappy place without your contributions.

So gather your books, place them on your bookshelves, and glory in the sight of your own library—

Your personal place of joy!

Challenge

Have you received a challenge? Has a circumstance in your life awoken a desire or a dream?

How will you handle this enigma?

Do you have the courage to bring about this change—to take a risk, to leave the safety of your life and venture forward toward that goal?

Be a risk-taker. What do you have to lose? Contemplate instead, *What do I have to gain?* Success or failure, one never knows what it might be.

The future we cannot see! The challenge is like a flag snapping in the wind, constantly drawing attention.

Investigate your challenge, talk to others who have taken a chance, read all the pertinent facts that give you knowledge, analyze the time and effort it will take to be successful, and then step off the cliff.

No matter what happens, you had the courage to try.

Clouds

As you wake in the morning, do you glance out the window to look at the sky?

Have you given much thought to the power of the clouds and how they affect our moods?

Today, the clouds are dark, some black, some gray, covering the whole sky.

No patches of sun anywhere to be seen, a picture to be sure. Does it make you say, "Another gloomy day to be had"?

But on the days when we look up and see only blue sky with a few fluffy clouds picturesquely floating by, our spirits are light, and smiles come easily to our faces.

Then there are the days when it is almost even—half blue and half clouds—so whatever our personality, one will see gloom, and others see joy.

Clouds and their power, do you see it?

No matter what the clouds show for today, let us be thankful that we can share one more of the daily glories that God bestows on us all!

Daffodils

Spring is here, according to the calendar.

The trouble is, cold days make us shiver, rain blasts the landscape, and snow has been known to blanket the ground.

Through all this, one sturdy and beautiful flower pushes its way through the ground.

No matter what it will find, the daffodil will not be deterred.

The beautiful yellow flowers, often found in groups, color our gardens, the paths we walk, and the banks by the roadside.

The color is so brilliant that you can see from afar the masses of yellow heads and petals beckoning us toward them.

This is the first flower of spring that creates such a spectacular image.

Amazingly, daffodils live for weeks, and even when nature does her worst, they emerge standing proud, yellow as the sun, giving us the pleasure of the perfect spring flower.

Darkness

The sun is bright, the breeze mild, the flowers colorful: All is well.
People drive by, living their lives, enjoying their jobs, looking
forward to the time spent with their families.

And I am here, locked in the darkness, afraid to leave my room.

Secure in the protection of my four walls.

Comfortable in the possessions that are my security, knowing
that I don't have to share, don't have to listen to others' problems
or concerns, engrossed in my own world, free of obligations or
difficulties.

But am I happy in this state? Am I satisfied with this life?

This life that friends and family keep trying to pull me out of.

They say it's because they love me.

Can I trust those friends and family?

Can I take the step necessary to change my life?

Dear God, give me the strength.

Day Needs Night

In this way, nature and the residents of this planet are similar.

For one minute, consider what composes our days.

The world of ours is a boiling kettle, waiting to overflow.

The changeable weather, the endless traffic, and commotion; the ceaseless movement of thousands of people. No break from the constant activity.

Then our workdays end, and our evenings begin with dinner, movies, homework, meetings, and best of all, the sharing of the joys and problems of the day.

Now consider how nature is also ready for the nighttime.

Animals who do their hunting at night, when it is safe to move across the terrain; others curl up in their nests and caves.

The fauna has a break from the invasion of trampling human feet.

As the world outside slows, our world inside acts accordingly.

A time for us to take a break, slow down, succumb to sleep; the dark snuggles us in its arms!

The world and all who live in it need this precious time of calmness, stillness, and quiet.

God's gift of peace to nature and humans!

Dignity

The essential dignity of a man is imperative to his survival.

Do not abuse it you employer, you stranger, you parent, you son.

Rob a human of his dignity, and you leave him naked, alone with no defense, making him a ship without a rudder.

March to the steps of your purpose.

Existence is your goal.

Existence with dignity!

Look beyond, friend, beyond black, yellow, or white.

Look to a soul,

A colorful soul filled with dignity.

Dreams

What are your dreams? Are they scary, happy, or sad?

Are you a participant, or is someone else the main character in your dream?

Do you wake up shaking and afraid from your dream, scared to go back to sleep as you don't want to resume your thoughts, or are your dreams happy and full of those you love having fun-filled adventures?

Do you remember your dream, or is it a jumble of thoughts with no rhyme or reason? A confusion of places with no significance to your life whatsoever?

What I hate the most is having a great dream, but I can't remember the details. So be prepared. Have paper and pen ready, and write out your dream.

Keep it for prosperity!

Maybe it will encourage new paths for your life, new adventures waiting for you.

These are the dreams of your imagination!

Drifting into Worry

Do you find yourself worrying all the time,

Every detail, incident, plan, taking too much of your effort in

What do I do about this situation?

How do I handle the problem, bring success to the outcome: Not

to say that we shouldn't have goals; of course we should.

But do those goals take too much of your present day in worry,

stress, and negative feelings?

The past is done!

You cannot do anything about it except learn from your mistakes.

The future is out of reach.

Plan what you need to do, and then let it go, cut the line.

Enjoy today, this minute in time.

Enjoy the beauty around you,

Your friends, family, and home!

Today is yours.

Duty

When I hear the word *duty*, I think of young men and women called to serve.

Never having found a career, never finding the perfect mate, or if they have,

Never being able to enjoy precious time together.

And yet they go willingly, ready to protect the land they love.

We owe so much to those who sacrificed, who went to foreign lands to stem the tides of war.

Some returned to us; some never came home.

Do we realize and appreciate the sacrifices they made?

We will never have to face such a challenge as these young men and women had to,

Giving up the life that they looked forward to and having to live the life of terror every day.

We really can't imagine the stress of it all!

So in our thoughts and prayers, let us say, "Thank you."

Thank you to the men and women of the armed forces who gave all for you and me.

Failure

Do I help you? Alas, how I failed.

All my training, all my desire goes for naught as I let you down, my dear.

Dear Father in heaven, turn once more this failure to your glory.

And next time, Father, let me turn to you first so that you might work through me rather than patching up after me.

Fear

Blind as a bat, I move around in my cubicle.

Feelings resound and echo from my being, communicating my unworthiness.

I search for the door; finding none, I relinquish all.

And then I wake up, out of the darkness.

I find myself in another place, another time.

Where have I been, where am I going?

My world is not what it is supposed to be.

Why am I seemingly living in two locations?

I have to figure this out before it drives me to act irrationally.

First, I am going to document my actions.

When I awake in the morning, I will list the time, where I am, and what I am going to do for this day. I will list what time I go to bed and where I am.

I will do this for a week to see what happens.

Somehow this is giving me confidence.

This week is done; I have been in my home, only my home for this whole week.

I don't know what happened and why I was acting so irrationally. But it is done!

I accept what I have been given and thank God for the blessing.
I will live my life in joy and thankfulness, helping others when they are in need.
A gift of life, so live it fully.

Flowers

The joy of our lives!

The beauty that knows no bounds!

The source of pleasure that is accessible to all of us; whether we buy them or grow them, we can enjoy them.

They fit anywhere you want—on tabletops, in vases, in beds surrounding our houses, in pots both inside and outside.

They will be around us to give our spirits a lift.

So keep these flowers in sight, live in the beauty of color, the glorious scents that fill our senses, the panorama of miles upon miles of flowers growing in the wild.

One of the gifts of nature in God's domain!

Fly with Me

Fly with me, my beautiful butterfly.

Fly through the sun of summer, the clouds of autumn, the snow of winter.

Fly with the strength and courage that

God has given you.

Fly with the love and support of all who care for you.

Fly to the edge of the earth,

The end of time!

Forgiveness

Forgive? What for?

It is not for me to forgive.

I have carried this weight for too long.

What could take its place?

I have lost the reason, secured it away from thought.

I have piled on hundreds more reasons since then. I don't have to look for explanations; I throw them all together and bury them deeper.

It is convenient where I have placed them. Everything is secure there!

All my problems, all my hurts, all my failures, all the mistakes I may have made,

I do not have to think about them.

I do not have to acknowledge or hate the part I may have played.

Peace, you ask?

What is that?

I had it once, a long, long time ago.

Godfather

Have you heard the term, "a gentle soul"? Well, that was Godfather. All his working life, he helped to heal those whose lives were suddenly changed by the onset of illness.

He was a part of the hospital team that operated and changed the direction of a disease or

Injury so that healing could occur for his patient.

How many people did he set back on their paths? We will never know for sure, but thousands and thousands I would guess; individuals who were able to reclaim their personal and work lives.

And in his private life, he was always there to help, guide, and enjoy his family and friends.

He shared his home and his heart.

How privileged I was to have known him the short time that I did.

How privileged his family for all the years they shared.

His life was well lived!

Thank you for being the example, the beacon that we should emulate for being

A gentle soul.

God's Hands

As I drove this morning, I thanked my God for giving me one more day.

As looked up, I saw the amazing clouds.

The first layer, closest to earth, was filled with dark, dark clouds racing swiftly through the sky.

The cloud layer above, white as snow, perfectly still with breaks of sun in between.

Layers upon layers, humans are the same.

The outside layer showing what we want the world to see.

The inside layer carrying the stillness and beauty that God gave us but also carrying the turbulence, the strife that daily living brings about.

God's hands upon the earth for us to observe, for us to enjoy, for us to remember

His love for us each and every day!

God's Helper

For each day that we live
We are given the chance,
The chance to meet,
The chance to greet,
The chance to change a life that weeps,
The chance to calm a troubled heart.
Do you meet that challenge or turn away?
Do you think it will happen another day,
A day when you are prepared and feeling OK,
A day when you don't have plans and it suits your way?
God's way is to be your way.
God's needs are to be your needs.
When God asks, we obey.
So look for the chances; don't run away.
Do God's bidding each and every day,
In small and large ways, always his way.
For thus you will be God's helper here today.

Growing Old

How will you grow old?

Will it bring you unhappiness, complaints, and anxiety?

Or will you face it with an open attitude, actually not even recognizing your age in years, only the age in how you feel?

Ready to tackle new challenges, experience the world, and what it has to offer.

Extend your knowledge in a new field all for your enjoyment.

Be open to the glory of each and every day that you are given.

The choice is yours!

Grandchildren

A joy beyond words.

Enjoyment without responsibility!

It is not our obligation to teach, not our obligation to monitor, not our necessity to train.

We can lend a hand and share our knowledge, impart our wisdom, but only when the opportunity occurs.

We have the freedom to play, the latitude to share fun experiences, the joy of happiness in being together.

We watch as they grow, glowing in the pride of seeing them mature, loving the emerging personalities as they find their path through life.

The years slip by too quickly, and suddenly, they are adults ready to begin their adulthood.

How glorious has been this journey. Memories forever, never to be lost,

Always in our minds and hearts.

Our grandchildren.

Helping Others Helps You

Giving of yourself is an answer to the depression of the soul.

When we concentrate only on ourselves, our problems, our issues, our failures, we leave no room for love.

No room for sharing with another.

No room for helping ease the pain someone else might be experiencing.

No room for compassion and sympathy.

So open your heart and soul; sweep out your problems and think of another!

In helping that person, you might find the answer to whatever has been causing you pain.

You might find the answer staring you in the face.

The answer you have sought, brought to you by your unselfish act of caring for another.

Her Fingerprints Will Be on Your Life

Her touch of love through illness and pain,

Her laugh of joy at your accomplishments,

Her cry of sorrow when your life falls apart.

She will always be with you to share life's occurrences.

To prop you up when you just can't stand, to encourage you to try and try until you succeed.

The shoulder to cry on, the arms to hug you, the kiss to bless you.

How precious is this gift,

The gift of a mother's love!

Home Away from Home

Do you have a place of peace, a place that feels like home?

Not the original,

Your birthplace, or the substitutes where you have lived, the college dorm, or the first apartment when you left home.

This home away from home to me was the vacation paradise.

A home that we visited every year at least once or twice.

This beach house sitting by the ocean, so different, so exciting.

Everyone came, our time to enjoy each other without stress or obligations.

No schedules to hamper our fun. The time to sit on the porch and share our thoughts and bond once more.

Meals that came together with the help of everyone, some cooking, some cleaning.

Nights that we played games sitting around the dining room table, laughing and joking.

Memories that were made forever to form our life stories.

Our home away from home.

Hope, the Restoring of Hope

Have you lost the possibility of hope?

Are you negative to the degree that possibilities no longer exist?

Are you building a wall of negativity that cannot be breached?

It is in your hands to prevent this occurrence.

In your hands to rebuild your walls with massive windows that will allow the light to brighten the darkness.

The beam of hope enters your space, giving you the opportunity of believing, the hope of achievement, the hope of healing, and the joy of happiness.

So grab that beam, and take the opportunity to believe once more in hope.

I Lost My Job Today

Oh, they were very nice. It wasn't me, they said, but economics.

I'm standing on a cliff, looking down; a small wind will be able to blow me over.

What am I to do?

There weren't any rumors, speculations that something was amiss.

Nothing to give me a little warning to be able to prepare myself for my fate.

Everyone was stunned; there were more than just me.

Emotions tear through my body; I feel as though I could faint.

My legs are moving, I know not where.

I'm going, knowing that I have to get some air, see the sun shining above, feel the wind caressing my skin; nature that flows, no matter what.

Give me courage to face my life.

My problems aren't solved, but somehow, I know that I will go on, and I will succeed.

In Unity there is Strength

Alone, none of us were strong enough, but together, we did it.

Problems present themselves to us, small ones to major ones.

Problems that we may be able to solve ourselves to huge problems that take a magnitude of people to solve them.

Small as some may be, when we are trying to find answers, they seem monumental.

We must remember that unity is a gift to us, giving us the power of numerous minds working together to come up with the answers.

Giving us all the power of thought, ideas, and solutions to be shared, analyzed, and used if they are appropriate.

Working together, in harmony, sharing ideas and allowing the majority to rule for the betterment of all.

If we want to be strong in our own families, and if we want to be a strong nation, we need to be unified, working with each other to fix the problems that come our ways.

We will be an example of what can be!

Unity for all.

I Took a Walk

I took a walk through the autumn calm.

Through weeds so tall they formed a wall.

The grass-crushed pathway held hollows waiting to catch my unwary foot.

The crickets jumped with each step I took, a road to be covered, a little brook.

I sat and listened and looked.

I was the reflection!

I was the sky!

I danced over rocks!

I swept through the trees!

And then through the calm; a siren split the air.

Reality surfaced abruptly, bringing me back to where I sat.

Shaking off the visions, I rose and left this precious place.

Thanks to God for the beautiful world and for the wonderful visions that bring such a joyful walk.

Land of the Free

America, our homeland.

Do we realize how blessed we are to live in a country without civil unrest,

To live in a country relatively safe compared to the rest of the world,

To live in a country with the beauty of deserts, mountains, rivers, and lakes?

Cities filled with glorious architecture and picturesque towns alive with small-town activity.

A country that is so easy to travel within.

All the methods of transportation, good roads, buses available, or trains if you would prefer.

Or if you desire, flying is the fastest way to go.

To live in a country where you are free to speak your mind, to choose your political favorite, or even to be involved in politics yourself if you so desire.

A country that has never had a world war within its boundaries, so we have been blessed not to have to rebuild our cities.

What a blessing we have been given, so let's enjoy it.

Cherish the gifts, appreciate the freedoms we enjoy, and be thankful for all the opportunities we are given in

The land of the free.

What a marvelous gift to each and every one of us.

Layers

As I drove this morning, I thanked my God for giving me one more day.

As I looked up, I saw the wonderful clouds.

The first layer, closest to the earth, dark, dark clouds racing swiftly through the sky.

The second layer above, white as snow, perfectly still with breaks of sun in between.

Layer upon layer, humans are the same!

The outside layer showing what we want the world to see; the inside layer carrying the stillness and beauty that God gave us, but also carrying the turbulence, the strife that daily living brings about.

Each layer different but coexisting.

God's hand upon the earth for us to observe, for us to enjoy.

For us to remember his love each and every day.

Leaves

Ah, September: It is almost time for the kaleidoscope of color that turns our landscape into a rainbow.

Leaves that turn to yellow, orange, brown, and red, a medley of shades covering all the trees in our sight.

It is the ending of this year's panorama until the rebirth of spring.

Beginnings and endings, how blessed we are to have this cycle to enjoy.

So let's take a walk in the woods, a drive through a forest, a picnic in the park, and absorb the beauty of our surroundings.

And on the days when the wind has its way and blows through the trees, the leaves fall freely, the sky is filled with color; lift your eyes, and indulge in the sight.

Feel the sting as leaves hit your skin, shuffle your feet and hear the rustle as you walk through the piles that have gathered on the ground, and smell the unique odor in the air.

Spend time with the beauty of fall!

Let God In

You have worries that you cannot solve, you have problems that won't go away, you have paths that you can't decide which to take, so you ask God, "What shall I do?"

You pray and say, "Thank you, God, for hearing my prayers." And then, in the blink of an eye, you are back to worrying, back to agonizing over decisions, back to the frustration of the unknown.

You have asked God for his help, and then you have refused to let him in.

You have blocked all chance of his help, blocked individuals who he may have sent to listen and advise you. Blocked love and caring and help that he can bestow on you. Can you let it go?

Allow God to show his love for you. Let peace steal into your heart, replacing the worry and the frustration that dwells there, allowing yourself to be open to others, allowing yourself to help where help is needed, not locked away, ignoring all.

Peace in our souls bring comfort and joy.

It won't be easy.

We are so determined that peace and forgetting about our worries is a negative action and that we have to try and control the outcome.

That attitude will block God's desire to help.

Let him answer your prayer.

Let him guide your path as you have asked him to.

Let God in.

Light

Shine light on what you want to grow.

Think about this statement; it makes such good sense.

We know a flower can't grow to its full potential without light, and this applies to almost all plant life.

Think about applying this same principle to those around you; children, family, friends, coworkers, all could benefit from the power of light.

Light means attention!

Light means encouragement!

Light means devotion!

All of the help that we need in order to live a beneficial life, nothing too difficult: Keep it simple; nowhere does it specify how much light, so just keep it consistent.

We all need the daily light, all God's creatures.

Bring on the light.

Love

What is love?

How do we define it?

Love is companionship.

Love is kindness.

Love is caring.

Love is compassion.

All of these you bring to me!

A blessing at any age, but especially for me at this stage of my life.

So thank you for all; may I respond in kind.

Memories

Memories are the building blocks of life. They may be pleasant, they may be unhappy, but they all combine to create the picture of your journey.

Memories begin as our minds absorb and remember the occasion. From that moment on, we begin our life experiences.

Our childhood years of play, of discovery, of early learning with little responsibility.

We move on then to our teen years with all the joy of beginning to experience life, bringing us chores, a job and much more learning, wonderful friends, and the adulthood looming, waiting for us.

Next we choose our career paths; we choose the love of our life and begin settling into the routine that will be the rest of our life.

The memories that no one can take away from us, the one thing that belongs to us forever and ever.

So cherish those memories, remember them, share them with your children before they can be forgotten or lost in the busyness of life.

Write them down, document a life; only you can accomplish this.

A treasure that will be shared for future generations.

Your life!

Mistakes

The past and the future are not within our grasp.

We have today, this moment in time.

Learn from the past, and vow not to make the same mistakes.

There are so many examples given to us each and every day.

Books that show us the proper way to conduct ourselves, friends that make mistakes whom we can stand behind but also learn from their actions.

Movies and television shows that picture people acting in the worst possible ways, which also show the consequences of our behavior.

We will make mistakes—it is inevitable—but try to make them small and not hurtful to everyone you love.

This world of ours is not an easy world to live in, so be diligent through the years, store all the knowledge that you have accumulated, and use that information when you need to.

It is there, waiting to help you through the tough times, and we will all have those.

The past is our cushions, surrounding us with love and knowledge for our use.

Music

Music is one of the joys of life, bringing comfort and fulfillment whether you are an artist or one of the audience who listens.

Music brings peace in times of stress, happiness and smiles to sooth the spirit.

It brings memories of years gone by, counted in the songs of each generation. Songs that marked all our special occasions, never to be forgotten as they are the fabric of our lives.

Music takes us into another dimension, out of this world into the land of sound.

Our minds stop their churning, slow to a crawling pace, allowing us to drift and flow with the music up and down the emotional scale. Nothing can bring us the stillness of feeling as though we are asleep, lulled and cradled in the words and notes, only pulled back to reality when the music stops.

And then there is the music of jazz and rock and country that reaches out to us and energizes us. Makes us want to dance and express our joy in movement, in singing, or clapping to the beat.

It exhilarates us until we are filled with the sounds that burst through our veins.

All types of music for all types of people. Continue to fill your life with music; and to all of those who bring us music, thank you for the gift that you give to all of us.

My Friend, My Pet

You came to me purely by chance.

There were two dogs available that day at the shelter.

I chose you, or maybe I should say we chose each other.

The attraction was there. It was meant to be.

And so it began!

The joy of seeing each other after we had been apart, the thrill of the chase as we sprinted down a path, the comfort of love as we lay together side by side.

A future to look forward to, my pet and I.

My Home

My home, whose walls are vaults of memories.

My sanctuary from all the commotion of life, whose doors open to the warmth and love I need.

Where I feel peace and comfort as I step over the threshold and enter.

The memories of births, birthdays, holidays—such as Thanksgiving and Christmas—and family dinners.

The reminders of children's laughter, tears, successes, and failures.

The maturing and moving forward of these same children to lives of their own

And the acquisition of their own homes.

These walls have seen so much shared, so much, and now I am alone.

But never alone!

My Job

Late in life I found my job!

Will I leave it? "Never," I say.

Do I love it? Without a doubt.

I am a caregiver to those in need, ready to do what they require.

Support and caring to lessen their loads; I form a relationship, a friendship, a kinship to each and every one.

They become my family!

Did God bring me here, to this place in my life? Undoubtedly he did!

And so I pray that I might be open to anyone who needs help wherever and whenever that might be.

Negativity or Positivity

Negativity is a backbreaker in our lives. We didn't ask for it. We weren't searching for it.

It is a part of our lives, a part of our personalities.

The issue with negativity is that our lives can be governed by its presence. It can overwhelm and consume our thoughts and actions. While positivity can bring joy and self-satisfaction, negativity can bring despair and hopelessness. Since we all have pieces and parts of both of these traits, how can we strengthen ourselves to use these two diverse actions to our benefit?

Always remember there is a choice here!

At times in your life, you might not believe that it is possible, but you do control those actions.

You decide how to fight the negative.

You decide how to dwell in the positive.

Devise an action plan for those times when you feel yourself slipping into unhappiness.

Write it down—step by step—your goals and purposes.

Easy things to immediately engage yourself in, allowing your mind to carry you above the abyss.

Take control. It is *your* life.

Make it a good life, a fruitful and fulfilling one!

No Heat

The winds were blowing, gusts reaching sixty miles an hour or so the weatherman reported.

As I drove, I had to tightly grasp the steering wheel to keep the car on a straight path.

Walking was difficult as the wind grabbed my hair, my coat, and pulled all backward until I felt as though I would topple over.

The trees were swaying this way and that way, losing branches and leaves to the onslaught and power of the storm. Some losing the battle altogether and falling to the ground. Whatever was in their path—a car, a building, a fence, an animal, a human—nothing and no one had a chance. They were caught.

The poles along the road, the power stations cannot escape, and as in every storm, some lose this power inside their home.

That which we depend on, everything that controls our day-to-day living, is gone. Flip the switch, and nothing happens. No lights, no TVs, no heat. Everything that gives us a civilized life is gone.

How we don't appreciate until we don't have it any longer. Our home is a shell. We might as well

Leave; we can't utilize or enjoy it. It is dark and cold.

And then in a flash, the power comes back on, and we resume our lives.

Do we remember the blessings we enjoy, not just in the power that warms our homes but all
The blessings we are given?
Appreciate and be thankful because all can disappear in a heartbeat.

On the Road Again

I hear the call; I feel the restlessness; my feet are itching, it is time to go!

The road is waiting. I have done this before, this exploration of the country.

Do I go to the east or to the west; to the north or to the south?

Whichever way it is, the adventure will never be the same,

This joy in meeting new people, seeing new vistas, experiencing local foods, visiting the culture of each area.

I can feel the wind blowing through my hair, smell the odor of the road, hear the music bursting in the air; these are the memories I will cherish.

Do you take the challenge? Pack your bag, find a good map, and off you go.

Come join me, on the road again!

Optimism

They say that an optimistic person sees the world through rose-colored glasses.

And I say, "What's wrong with that?"

If we see the good in those who walk the path,

If we see the beauty in the world around us,

If we block the negative in thought and deed,

We will make the world a better place.

Negativism fosters unease, allows hope to be eradicated, causes darkness to shadow our days, sees unhappiness in every situation.

If you had a choice, which would you rather exhibit,

The joy of optimism or the despair of negativism?

Make your choice!

It is in your hands.

Our Pasts

What do we do with our pasts?

Do we wrap them all up and bury them deep, so we aren't bothered by them?

Or do we use the past as a learning tool for the future?

One thing that might help our decision is that our minds are remarkable parts of our bodies.

Do we forget something that took us months and years to learn?

Do we forget anything that might help us with the future?

So I believe that the answer is very clear to see.

We need the past to handle the future.

Forgive yourself for any past mistakes, and use the knowledge that you were given to make your present a more pleasant and satisfying place to be.

Learn from the past, and learn from today.

Learning never stops!

Our Restaurant

We were both working, my husband and I, he at a bank, and I at a hospital when he decided that he wanted to accomplish his dream and open a restaurant. We owned a house that we rented out which became a small, comfortable, homey Italian restaurant.

A start of a new and wonderful experience in our lives. So we remodeled and turned that house into a family-style eating experience. For twenty-eight years, it was our destination. All our children were employed. The year we opened, our oldest daughter graduated from high school, and she and her friends all waitressed. Our son did all the odd jobs and even cooked at times. Our youngest daughter cooked one whole summer and filled in as necessary.

It was a family-friendly location. We met locals and followed their lives, making friends, enjoying the stories of their lives, and watching their families grow. We enjoyed the people who worked for us as they became family.

A small business has its challenges, but the rewards are unbelievable. We didn't make a lot of money, but we sure enjoyed the food. So if the chance should present itself,

Take the leap, check the possibilities of what life can offer and what we can offer in return.

So to all our family, friends, and customers, thank you for becoming a part of Reggie's history.

Patience

I do believe that when it comes to patience, some people are given a personality that seems naturally more patient and off course; the opposite are those who lose that trait rather quickly.

This observation only points out the necessity that we stop and analyze our actions.

Life is so full, we all keep so busy that we don't take the time to study ourselves, our actions, our needs.

We are so involved in loving and caring for our families, in working hard at a job that is necessary for our living that we don't look introspectively at who we are becoming.

Peace, the goal for all of us is lurking in the shadows.

Happiness, a gift, waits as we struggle with daily issues.

Patience seems to be hiding behind a darkening cloud.

It's time to take care of ourselves, evaluate the necessities, eliminate the unnecessary, take charge of our lives so that we can put some peace back in our existence; so that we can enjoy the time that we have been given with less stress and more understanding of ourselves.

People

Have you ever sat in a mall and watched all the people, the sizes, the shapes, the heights, and the weights?

The faces, each one different, hundreds, thousands, none alike. Some happy, smiling, laughing; some scowling and unhappy, some in a hurry, others leisurely strolling along.

What are their lives comprised of: happiness and sadness, hope and despair?

All of us facing trials and tribulations, sorrow and pain. All of us facing joy and satisfaction, peace and calm.

Times of sorrow, times of joy.

No matter our color, nationality, religion or age,

Under the skin, we are all the same.

Personality

What personality are you? Are you more quiet, sitting back and listening to all that happens around you?

Or are you the person who is in the front of the circle, leading the pack in all that occurs?

Is there a right or wrong way to be?

Absolutely not!

Most important for all of us is that we trust the personality that we are.

Be true to ourselves.

Enjoy who you have become.

For in this world of ours, there is room for all.

There is a necessity for all types and personalities.

What would the world be like if we were all the same?

I know that sometimes we see that person who is directly opposite of us and think, *I wish I could be a little more like that.*

Well, try it and see.

Do you feel comfortable in those shoes, or are you an actor in a play?

Be yourself; trust in yourself.

People who know you love the person you are.

Relish that gift, and travel your path!

Possibilities

Life is full of possibilities, from birth to death.

They lie before us, waiting to be noticed, begging to be utilized.

Do we ignore them, or do we claim all the opportunities that God gives us?

What we do with these gifts is up to us.

Use them or lose them as the saying goes!

Each day that we are given, be observant.

Can we make it a goal?

Today I will watch!

Today I will claim!

Today I will make the dream come true.

Prayers

I see you sitting there, a stranger to me.

Yet, you are in pain, confused; I sense it in my being.

I smile, you reply. No more is possible.

But for today, my prayers are yours.

Someone will come to give you help.

To that end, I pray.

Poems

The whispers of your heart!

The desire to verbalize an action observed, a spoken word shared between

Individuals, the beauty of nature given to us daily, the joy of love, all waiting to be shared through the gift of words.

Words that can encourage us, stimulate us, and give us peace and security.

Poetry can reach the middle of your heart: Once there, it will spread its peace throughout your system.

In a life that is full of decisions, responsibilities, problems, and constant upheavals,

we need help to keep us calm and motivated, willing and wanting to accomplish all the goals that we have set for ourselves.

So let us find a poem that speaks to our hearts, place it where we can see it each and every day, and go forward with thankfulness for the lives we have been given.

Respect for Differences

You have heard it said that if we were all the same, the world would be a strange place.

Difference is what makes individuals who they are.

Differences in looks and attitudes, differences in interests, wants, and needs.

But with these differences comes an obligation for each of us—
the obligation of respect—for in order to live a peaceful life, we need to respect the differences of others.

We need for each person in this world to be allowed to make their own choices, right or wrong, to find their own paths, straight or crooked.

We don't need to agree with their choices, but we do need to respect the right of choice for each individual. In doing so, we give up the desire of trying to change others. A task that is impossible and not our duty or our judgment to make.

Let us put that task in the hands of God and accept for ourselves the task of recognizing respect for all who live in this world with us.

Rudeness

Is it contagious? Does hearing rudeness by another prompt us to answer in kind?

Does it give us the freedom to speak out of turn, to hurt another with words that, once spoken, cannot be retrieved?

Do we not have an obligation to be as pleasant as we can, to make the atmosphere

Around us calm and peaceful, allowing all to feel in control?

Can we ignore the individual who uses rudeness to gain attention, who tries

To draw us into confrontation? Thereby giving themselves satisfaction from the disruption that occurs. Remember, there are times when we are not feeling our best—we did not sleep well, we had an argument with a loved one, someone was driving irrationally, we forgot an obligation that we had promised to keep; all circumstances that test our patience.

At these times, can we draw a deep breath and talk to ourselves? No one else is at fault for our bad feelings, and taking it out on others will not make us feel better.

The opposite will happen, and we will feel worse.

So be silent! Keep to yourself because your mood will change. You know it will.

And your world as you know it will not be disturbed by your actions and behavior.

Rudeness will be squelched; you will have done your part to make it so!

Should Have Done It Life

Don't let your life be a "Should have done it life."

When you look back at the close of your life, will you be able to say, "I did it all"?

When the chances occur, do you follow your dreams?

Do you take the risks, debating the problems but accepting no defeat?

Is your mind attuned to what could be, believing in yourself and what accomplishments can be had?

There might be disappointments, even failures, at times, but if you never try, there won't be failure. But there won't be successes either.

Better to try and fail than never to try at all.

Be ready to recognize the path to be traveled.

Be willing to accept help!

Don't be proud or a know-it-all; we all need a helping hand.

Be joyous and proud of yourself so that you will never have to say that you had a

Should have done it life.

Silver Lining

Have you experienced a silver lining, or is it still a dream that floats before you?

A silver lining doesn't have to be a huge miraculous occurrence; it can be a small blessing amid a big problem.

In each situation that we encounter, if we are blessed, we will look for the silver lining,

The answer to a problem that is looming over us, making each day a trial.

A hopeless situation that has no answer we can see, only pulling us down and down into deeper depression, wiping out all the pleasure in our lives.

Making each day one that we don't want to experience.

What we are doing is blocking our path to our silver linings.

They are there, waiting for us to break through all the blackness.

It takes courage and determination to work out this problem that is holding us prisoner, realizing that the darkness can be removed if we work at it and have faith.

The light of the silver lining is shining brightly, showing us the path to take.

So be determined and brave.

Reach toward the light, and fight through the problems until you reach the

        The silver lining.

Spring Cleaning

The yard is a mess!

Winter has done her damage.

Leaves and tree limbs are all over, littering the grass from one end to the other. Dead plants lie in the flower beds, giving them a dreary look. Trees need trimming, shrubs need shaping, beds need edging. Our yards are ready and waiting for the love and care that we will give them. Each day I look out the window and say to myself, "Today. What do you think?" And of course, it doesn't happen fast enough.

But the day will come, and out I will rush, ready to rake, dig, cut, and trim.

The love of being outside, breathing in the fresh air, planning the flowers I want to plant, replacing those that died, and adding new colors and shapes that I have discovered.

The joy of the garden!

What greater gift can I receive?

Springtime

How we look forward to the beauty of spring!

The weakening of the cold and bluster.

The feeling of the breeze that alerts us to the warmth to come.

The pushing through the cold earth of the bulbs, tulips, daffodils, snowdrops, and hyacinths, showing us the strength and beauty to come.

The birds who have flown away to avoid the cold returning to us in their search for nests for the summer births of their fledglings.

The grass beginning to poke through the leaves and dirt that bury all of their greenery over the winter.

All the harbingers of the summer to come.

We can start planning our gardens; the vegetables, flowers, fruit, all we want to plant in just a little while.

The joy to come.

Solitude

When I am alone, my soul reaches to my heavenly Father.

He touches my spirit and rejuvenates my faith. I am his to use.

Cease your struggling, your willfulness; listen to your soul.

He cannot speak to you while you struggle.

He cannot speak to you when you direct your thoughts.

Be still, and reflect on his wonders—

The power of the wind, the glory of the sky, the majesty of a mountain.

His presence is around you. Can you not see?

Love from a friend who comforts us in sorrow.

Help from a stranger who ministers in sickness.

The touch of a loved one.

Be still, and feel his love.

Strength

Do you know that person with strength?

Through thick and thin, they handle it all with dignity, determination, courage, and fortitude no matter the cause.

Their attitude doesn't change, always positive, forgetting the past, dwelling on the present.

Have you met the individual who inspires you to become a better person, a kinder person, one with empathy for all?

A light shining for all to see!

Follow that light, and become the person of strength that you were meant to be.

Take Me Up

Take me up to those who wait, to those who have gone before.

Although I sorrow for those I leave, I know the time is right for me.

My life has been a glorious one with family and friends and abounding love.

I have spent my time trying to make life better for all around me.

I have enjoyed the beauty of the world God gave us.

And now, my job is done.

My path has a gate waiting for me.

I am ready and waiting.

Take me up!

The Beauty Salon

It's the place where women can go to restore their beauty and grace, where beauticians fix their hair, their nails, and their facial makeup. A salon dedicated to boosting their confidence, reclaiming their natural good looks and charm.

An hour or so, and we will be prepared to meet the world for another week.

All the problems, the stress of life, are forgotten during that time of someone else caring for us.

Thanks to all who labor for us so we keep looking our best.

Thanks to our beauty salon for providing the facility and the equipment to make our dreams come true.

Take Time

Take time to think.

It is the source of power.

Take time to read.

It is the foundation of wisdom.

Take time to pray.

It is the greatest power on earth.

Take time to love and be loved.

It is God's gift, given to you to share.

The Animals in Our Lives

Our pets who love us unconditionally,

Who share our happiness and pain by their presence beside us,

They never let us down; they are waiting by the door for us to come home whenever we go out.

They sleep when we sleep and are ready to start the day with us in the morning.

They share our sorrows and pain with the closeness and stillness as they lay beside us, giving us the comfort of their bodies.

When we go out for a walk, their happiness—which consists of jumping, spinning

In circles, and dancing on the paths—makes us try to keep up with them, giving us a good workout too, which is a benefit to our health.

Rusty, Baron. Callaway, Whitey, Annabelle, Sammy, Buddy, Chloe, and Bailey, all dogs in our lives.

Different breeds, different sizes, different colors, but all loved as members of our family.

So thank you for all you give to us.

Blessings over and over again for the love from the animals in our lives!

The Blue Moon

The blue moon shone in the sky, illuminated as if it had a spotlight shining from behind.

The clouds were lacy balls that captured the moon and then pushed through to escape to the other side.

The blue moon occurs when there are two full moons in a month. A treat to enjoy because of its rarity, occurring only every two to three years.

The beams fell on the sidewalk by my door, lighting the area with a soft glow so that I could see each brick, each bush, each flower as though it were daylight.

God's gift for today!

What will tomorrow's gift be? It is for you to discover!

Seek and you will find.

The Body

What an amazing gift God has given us in this body of ours.

We have all experienced the healing of cuts, the bruises that fade, the bones that knit together after the breaks, the curing of infections, the muscles that recover from a strain.

Do we know the power of this gift of healing? It will always be with us when the need arises, but do we utilize and assist our bodies in this process, or do we just take this gift for granted?

Physicians are aware of the benefit of a positive attitude to bring healing for whatever

Illness or disease we are facing.

Can we assist the medical staff with hope and positiveness to help bring about the cure that they wish for us?

No one wants it more than us, so do your part.

Concentrate on the positive.

Accomplish the possible,

the healing of our bodies.

The Colors of Autumn

As I drove down the road on a bright sunny day, I was looking at the vista before me but not really seeing it.

Suddenly, the sight invaded my senses, and I realized the green was almost gone, dominated by the colors of autumn.

The sun making golds, reds, and oranges of the leaves filled my vision. From the tops of the trees to the ground below, all was color sparkling with joy.

The ground, usually lawns of green, were filled with leaves, some scattered, others in piles waiting to be picked up, all making a golden blanket completing the picture of color.

In the middle of the road, two lines stretch forward, painted a deep yellow as though an artist needed the color to complement this picture.

Bushes of bright red nestled beside the houses, completing the layers of color.

From the top to middle to ground,

All a colored panorama.

What a glorious sight.

The Enemy Within

Do we concentrate so much on the enemy that we can't see that we dismiss the enemy within,

An enemy that nags and criticizes constantly?

An enemy that breaks down our confidence and leaves us afraid to move forward.

An enemy that takes away desire to succeed and leaves us a pile of ashes inside, burnt to nothing.

Can we fight this bleakness, clean the ashes away, allow warmth and light to fill the space where negativity reigned?

No one deserves this enemy. This enemy that destroys the potential that is yours and yours alone.

There is one person who can change this pattern, and that person is you.

Fill the space with hope, goals, plans, and confidence in yourself.

There will be no room for

The enemy within.

The Family Name

Each of us has a family name given to us once, our birth name.
The name is a precious gift that for generation after generation has been treasured and honored.
A name that once stained can never be corrected.
For whoever brings disgrace to that name will be remembered by future generations as the individual who brought shame to the legacy.
Do you want to be the one who fulfills this prophecy, tarnishing all the talented, honest, upright lives that previously shared your family name?
Think about it before you commit a foolish act.
Is this how you want to be remembered—with sadness, shame, and disgust?
Or would you like to be remembered as someone who contributed to the world they lived in?
You don't have to be rich or famous; more important, could you be remembered as someone who cared, who loved their family, and lived their life to make their world a better place?
The true legacy of a family name.

The Gift of Love

Love, how does it come to you?

In a flashing, blinding light, or does it creep up slowly, almost without your knowing?

Does it knock you in the head, or does it grow as you learn to know this new friend?

Is there a right or wrong way? Absolutely not!

Love for each of us comes in different ways and at different times.

It fills our hearts with joy and happiness. Gives us smiles when no one is around, a warm glow that makes our breath catch and tears come to our eyes.

A longing to be with this special person twenty-four hours a day, to share our pasts, our problems, and our successes.

To share our future dreams as we have never shared before, completely and without fear or reservation.

If this love comes to you, cherish the gift you have been given.

The gift of love.

The Power of the Mind

Do we realize the power of the mind,

What we can accomplish if we put that power to work to accomplish our goals?

This won't come easily or quickly.

It takes determination and time to bring about the answers that we are looking for.

It takes dedication to our goals, a straight path with no exits.

What we have to remember is that we have the power of our minds working for us.

So take the time to find a quiet, secure place where we won't be disturbed.

A place where we can work and lay out the decisions that we have to make.

Hopefully, we will always find the best solution, but don't count on that.

All we can do is study the situation and do what seems the right thing to do.

This will give us the satisfaction of our best efforts.

The Little Blessings

Often in life, we look too high for huge blessings that will change our life paths. Nothing small or insignificant for us; we want the miracle that will burst into flame and change our lives.

In so doing, we overlook the small blessings that we have been given each and every day. These miracles are before our eyes, overlooked all too often. Too obvious to make an impression on our brains.

The skeptic that I am, I ask, "What are those blessings that I am ignoring?" I'm thankful for all that comes my way, so where am I failing?

Blessings began when God first went to the lowly shepherds and told them he was sending his Son, Jesus, to us, not to the high clergy, wealthy, or intellectually brilliant but the lowest in the land. So let's start at the beginning, put our thinking caps on, and name all those small miracles.

The beautiful changing nature that gives us vistas beyond compare; rain, sun, snow, wind, all the changing climates. Flowers in abundance with colors of the rainbow. A smile given to us by a stranger, a helping hand when we most need it but couldn't find the courage to ask. A child's smile freely given in their innocence. And most of all, love given unconditionally.

Small blessings but life-changing the moment we receive them.

So keep your heart and mind open, waiting for God's blessing.

The Playhouse

I built the playhouse for my grandchildren, or so I told myself.
And mostly it was true, but a part of this goal, I must admit, was
for me.
I had the pleasure of choosing the wallpaper, the carpeting, the
furniture all to make it homey.
It was and is a place of solitude, away from all the hustle and bustle
of my daily life.
I go inside, and all is quiet, pretty, and peaceful; a place to take my
book and sit and read.
No TV, computer, or phone—although sometimes I do take my
phone.
I can't explain the difference of this space. It's just a room, but not
just a room as I am totally alone. When I look out the windows,
I am in my garden, tucked away among the trees and the flowers.
A place of comfort, solitude, and peace.
What a blessing it brings to me.
My lovely little playhouse!

The Storm

The storm, it was coming. Days away, the weatherman said.
Gathering strength as it slowly moved toward the land.
The speed of the storm gave it plenty of time to reach a level 4, a
very dangerous level.
Our home away from home was in its direct path, and on top of that
tragedy, the storm was named Florence, my middle name.
As we watch the news and listen to the reports, worry becomes
A constant companion.
Three or four more days go by, and the eye of the storm moves closer.
But miracle of all miracles, it drops to a level 2, still dangerous but
maybe a little less.
It approaches land, drops south, and hits the land.
Of course, everyone has been evacuated, so there is no one to tell
you the results.
A couple of days go by, and finally, a few pictures are posted on
Facebook and
In the paper; not enough for peace of mind, but a little reassurance.
Finally, they are allowing reentry.
The storm has moved on.
My son and grandson are on their way to North Carolina to check
out the situation.

We have been blessed; some roof damage, but our home away from home is still standing there to greet us for another memory-filled vacation.

Our oasis in the storm of life.

The Sun

The sun rose as usual, grabbed the land, and shone its golden rays into the fluffy clouds that nestled in the blue sky.

What a wondrous phenomenon to behold, and one that we take for granted.

The sun, our sustainer, without who all living creatures would not live as we know them now.

The sun that gives us light to bring us out of the darkness to begin each day. And though the sun may hide some days. It is still there, waiting for the opportunity to peak out at us.

What does the sun give to us?

First of all, a beauty with no comparison and then nourishment for all the land to sustain growth

In the forests, the flower beds. The vegetable plots, the bushes, and trees that surround our homes, giving them strength unconditionally each and every day.

At night, as the sun settles into the horizon, it gives us rest.

The rest that allows us to continue our lives.

The peace of the night awaiting the sun's birth with a new start, a new day!

The Trees of Winter

Finally, the evergreen is the king. Gone are all the leaves that decorate the trees, leaving tall, brown statues in the ground.

Now our sight is filled with the majestic evergreen.

Each branch beautiful in its shape of thick fur so thick that nests can hide; so thick that squirrels and birds can snuggle within the greenery.

The evergreen, which gives us one of our most precious memories, the Christmas tree. Decorated with ornaments, lights, tinsel, and icicles, the accumulation of a lifetime of remembrances.

Cities, towns, streets, houses all decorate their evergreens to make a fairyland of our environment.

What would we do without our evergreen tree.

What would our Christmas be?

I sit and look at an evergreen tree that has grown to be eighty feet tall but which was once our Christmas tree.

Bless you, evergreen, for your beauty today and in the future.

The Yardstick

The yardstick we use for others will be the yardstick used for us.

Therefore, if we treat others with unkindness, we can expect the same.

If we treat others with no respect or dignity, we can expect the same.

It is so simple as the Bible says, "Do unto others as you would have others do unto you."

Have we forgotten this proverb?

Does our life of instant, online communication take away the fear of retribution, the fear of discovery when we know that we are not acting as we should?

The knowledge that no one knows what we are doing and thus, no one will know if we have sinned.

Might I say, "Do not count on that."

Keep your yardstick on the positive side, and

All will be well.

To My Inspiration

Have you ever met an individual who was an inspiration to you?

A person with determination, a true kindness, and friend to many.

A person who led but didn't push, made themselves available but didn't interfere.

A friend who cared and reached out to any and all when times were tough.

An avid lover of landscape design, agricultural institutions, botanical gardens, bird life, and natural history.

What an example for us.

Look at that life, and emulate the examples that were meant for you.

And in so doing, become the person that others will emulate!

To Sue

A spark left the earth today.

A life of courage and strength displayed for all to see.

A life of pain and discomfort every minute of every day, and yet, she handled it with grace.

She always looked her best, always did her best to be a friend.

And friends she had! Thank you, God, for the friends as they supported her, loved her, gave her courage and companionship in the last months of her life.

I stand back and look at a life well-lived.

And I vow that I shall try to emulate this example of a life truly and beautifully led.

Travel

What a delight if you might have the chance to take a flight
To see new lands and famous sights, thousands of years of struggles
and successes.
The memories left in buildings, statues, and art.
Each country proud of their homeland and what they have
contributed to the history of the world.
To see buildings that are thousands of years old, still standing, a
monument to man's determination and love.
Each country different in its own way, but the common thread for
all is "the people"; no matter what country, what language, people
are the same.
I think that we don't appreciate ourselves enough. Don't realize the
goodness, the fun, the loving spirit that we find as we travel from
one border to another.
People living their lives each day in much the same way: working,
having families, sharing the joy of "God's world."
We are all one: Let us not forget this simple fact.
Wherever we may live,
Let us give thanks and protect this beautiful world that we inhabit.

Watching over You

As you lie in your bed for rest,

I will watch over you.

As you endure the pain, the frustration, the indecision,

I will watch over you.

The path of life brings all to us—the glories, the happiness, the successes, the sorrows, and the need for love.

And through it all, I will watch over you,

Until the day that I will call and ask you to come and watch over me.

Winter in the North

Winter, when all the land takes a rest.

When flowers cocoon under the earth and take a siesta before the warmth returns.

The trees lose the protection of their leaves and are bare to the elements.

Animals hibernate in small hollows or burrow into the earth to protect themselves from the weather.

A time for the forests to have less visitors; only those individuals who love the winter scene will venture into its arms.

Our hardy birds—such as robins, woodpeckers, English sparrows, and juncos—to name a few who don't migrate but stay with us through the winter.

We leave the summer green, the autumn reds, golds, and browns and welcome the pristine white.

Snowflakes flying through the air, covering everything from top to bottom with a blanket of white,

As beautiful in its own way as the seasons that have just passed.

The flow of nature, a wonder to behold.

World of White

I woke up this morning to a world of white, inches of snow snuggling in the corners of the buildings, lying on the branches of the shrubs, covering the foliage that surrounds our house.

Nothing has disturbed this beautiful panorama, neither the wind nor the sun.

Footprints fill the landscape with all animals and humans leaving their marks in the snow.

All the dirt and roots are covered in white, so that all is the same, with no delineation.

How long can it last, this pristine picture, this vista of peace and beauty?

Take a picture with your eyes; store it away in your vault of memories.

It will be with you forever to reflect upon when you need comforting.

And now the snow is falling again, small white flakes added to the layers.

And as I drive, just ahead of me is a fir tree decorated with small bulbs of all colors.

A beacon in my beautiful world of white.

Printed in the United States
by Baker & Taylor Publisher Services